April Fool!

"Do you know what day it is today?" said Mum.

"Yes, I do," said Michael. "It's April Fools' Day."

"Don't let people fool you then,"
said Mum.

"I won't," said Michael.
And off he went to school.

"Michael, Michael, there's a tiger right behind you!"

"Don't be silly," said Michael. "I know it's April Fools' Day and I won't look. So there!"

5

"Michael, Michael, now there's a witch right behind you!"

"Don't be silly," said Michael. "I know it's April Fools' Day and I won't look. So there!"

"Michael, Michael, now there's a bear right behind you!"

"Don't be silly," said Michael. "I know it's April Fools' Day and I won't look. So there!"

9

"Michael, Michael, now there's a robber right behind you!"

"Don't be silly," said Michael. "I know it's April Fools' Day and I won't look. So there!"

"Michael, Michael, now there's a wolf right behind you!"

"Don't be silly," said Michael. "I know it's April Fools' Day and I won't look. So there!"

13

"Michael, Michael, now there's a Grumble right behind you!"

"Don't be silly," said Michael. "I know it's April Fools' Day and I won't look. So there!"

"Michael, Michael, now there's a ghost right behind you!"

"Don't be silly," said Michael. "I know it's April Fools' Day and I won't look. So there!"

17

"Michael, Michael, now there's an ELEPHANT right behind you!"

"Don't be silly," said Michael. "I know it's April Fools' Day and I WON'T LOOK. SO THERE!"

19

"Hello, Michael.
I see some friends have come to
school with you today."

21

22